Farm Crops

by Althea

pictures by Jacqueline Wood

Published by
Dinosaur Publications

Most of the food you see in this picture is grown on farms and delivered direct to supermarkets.

peas

broad beans

French beans

Some foods go straight to factories.
Lots of peas and beans are sent to
freezing or canning factories.
Even sugar is a farm crop.
It is made from juice extracted from
sugar beet or from imported sugar cane.

The farmer plants different crops in
the field each year. This helps to stop
plants from getting diseases.
All these vegetables grow under
the ground.

leek

swede

onion

sugar beet

parsnip

radish

carrot

The farmer is lifting potatoes from the ground with a harvesting machine.

Many farmers grow lots of different food crops and some people grow food in their gardens or on allotments.

The potato plant has underground tubers which grow into potatoes

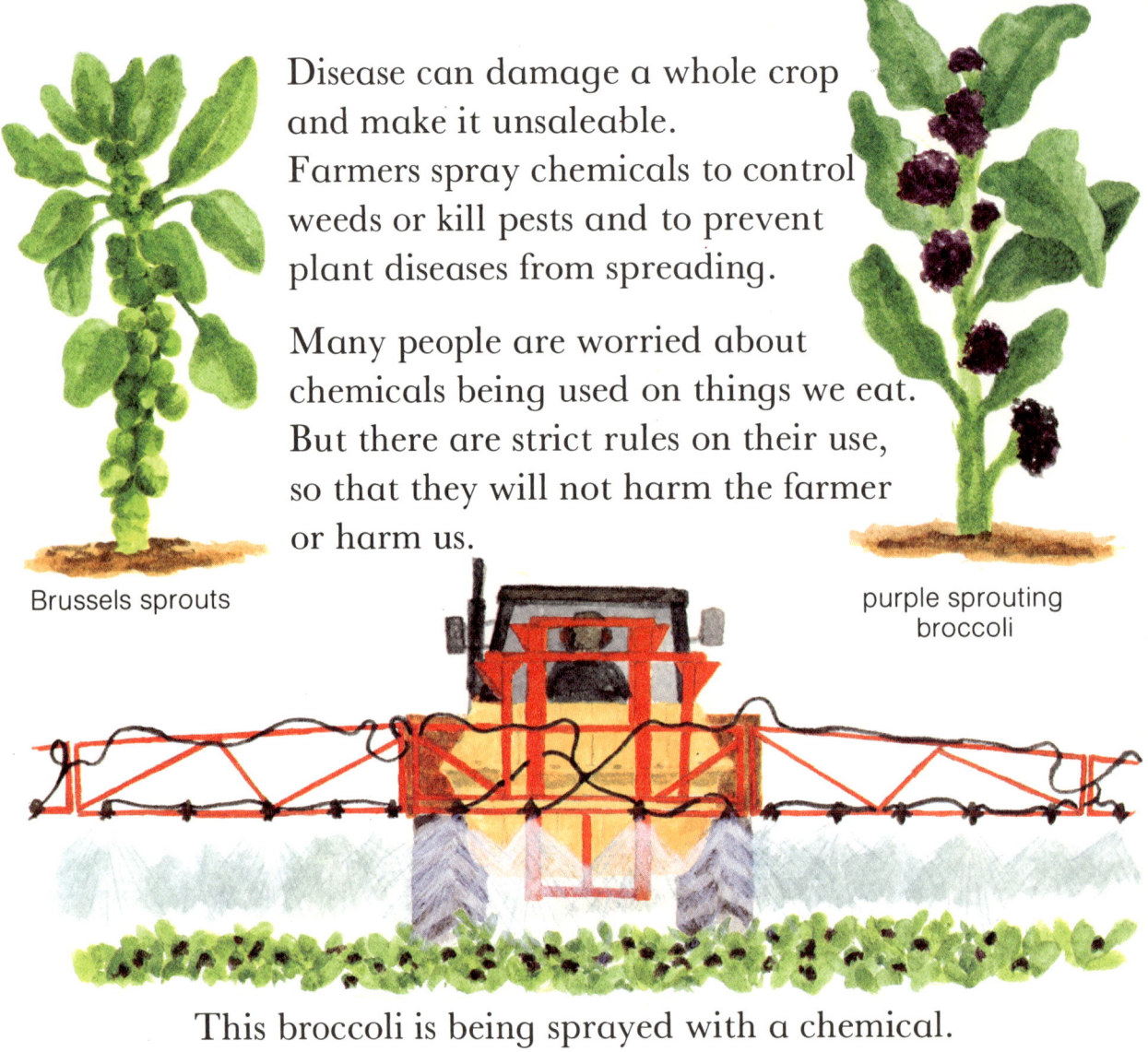

Disease can damage a whole crop
and make it unsaleable.
Farmers spray chemicals to control
weeds or kill pests and to prevent
plant diseases from spreading.

Many people are worried about
chemicals being used on things we eat.
But there are strict rules on their use,
so that they will not harm the farmer
or harm us.

Brussels sprouts

purple sprouting
broccoli

This broccoli is being sprayed with a chemical.
After spraying it won't be cut for three weeks
so people are in no danger from the chemicals.

It would be difficult to grow enough food for everyone without using chemicals, but some farmers would rather grow food without using them.
This is called organic farming.
Organically grown food is often more expensive but some people prefer it.

runner beans

cauliflower
Some farmers grow purple cauliflowers too!

spinach

cabbage

The fields of bright yellow flowers you see
in spring are growing oil seed rape.
When the flowers die the seed pods ripen.
The seeds are then crushed and oil for
cooking extracted from them.

oil seed rape

Fields of sunflowers are also grown for
the oil in their seeds.

In late summer golden fields of wheat, oats and barley will be ready for harvesting. Much of the grain will go to feed animals. Wheat is also used to make flour for bread and biscuits, oats to make cereals for breakfast and barley is used in making beer.

barley

wheat

oats

At this fruit farm strawberries are grown in the summer and there are fields of raspberry canes and currant bushes.
Some of the fruit is sold to a jam factory. People can also come and pick their own fruit, or buy it from the farm shop.
Perhaps they are going to make jam too.

blackcurrants

raspberries

strawberries

Later in the year, apples and pears
will be ready for picking.
They will be sent to the wholesale
fruit market, or packed and sold
direct to supermarkets.

Farms grow lots of different varieties of lettuce
to make salads look and taste more interesting.
Red lettuce look very colourful growing
in the field.

Lettuce are cut by hand and the people on the
back of the harvester pack and label them
ready for the supermarket.

iceberg lettuce

quattro stagioni

The lettuce will be taken to the packing shed and boxed.
The boxes of lettuce are then cooled and loaded on
to refrigerated lorries to keep them fresh for the shoppers.

Misshapen or wrong sized lettuce are chopped up and
used in salad packs, or bought by places like McDonald's
to put in hamburger rolls.

red oak leaf lettuce

lollo rosso

These lettuce are being grown in water, in a glasshouse, making them available all year round.

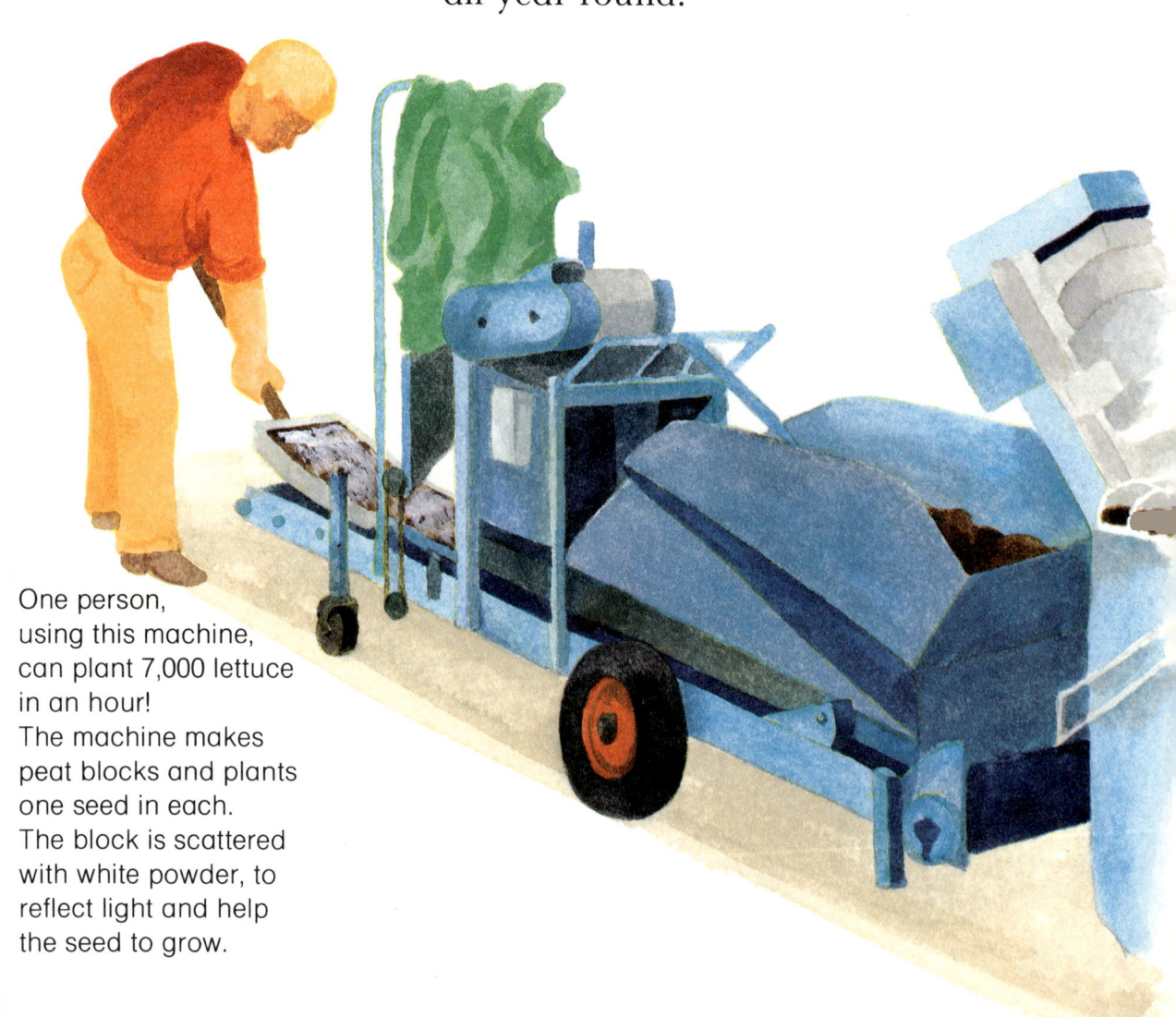

One person, using this machine, can plant 7,000 lettuce in an hour!
The machine makes peat blocks and plants one seed in each.
The block is scattered with white powder, to reflect light and help the seed to grow.

As soon as the lettuce start to grow the peat blocks
are placed in narrow channels of water.
Fertilizer is added to the water to help
the lettuce to grow.

The glasshouses are lit at night, when electricity
is cheaper, to encourage the lettuce to grow
quickly, and to protect them from frost.

These tomatoes and cucumbers are
being grown in glasshouses too,
so they will be ready to sell early
in the summer.

Instead of using chemicals,
some farmers buy and use tiny
predators called Orange Mites
to eat the Red Spider Mites
which damage their crops.

One Orange Mite will eat up to five adult or twenty young Red Spider Mites in a day!

Scientists are doing research to find predators which will eat the other pests which damage plants growing in glasshouses.

Watercress can only be farmed
where there is a very plentiful
supply of fresh running water.
It is grown on gravel beds and each
acre uses half a million gallons
of running water a day.
The watercress gets the food
it needs to grow from the water.

Watercress seedlings ready
for planting outside.

The water is warm when it comes
up from underground springs, so
it is possible for watercress to grow
all the year round.
When watercress flowers, people no longer
want to buy it, so seeds are planted
every ten days and the watercress is picked
before it flowers. The early summer crop
is sown in heated glasshouses in February.

Bunches of watercress
are picked by hand.
Packs of watercress can
be picked by machine.

This watercress
has flowered and
the seeds are
ripening in the pods.

Mushrooms double in size each day.
Shops and supermarkets mainly want small
cup and button mushrooms, so it is important
to start picking them as soon as they
are the right size or they will grow too
large and flat.
Some people prefer 'flats' because
they have more flavour.
Mushrooms grow from tiny spores
grown on sterilized grain.
The mushroom spawn is then mixed
into trays of clean compost.
In two weeks, the spawn grows,
turning the compost white.
It is then covered with a layer
of wet peat and chalk, and the trays
are taken to the warm growing room.

buttons

closed cups

open cups

In three weeks the first 'flush' of mushrooms
will be big enough to start picking.
Another 'flush' of mushrooms
will grow a week or so later.
After five weeks the main crop
will have finished, and the trays
are cleaned ready to start again.

Unlike other crops, mushrooms don't
need light to make them grow.

flats

This herb farmer sells packs of herbs to supermarkets, both here and in other countries.
She also supplies herbs to the food manufacturers, to use when cooking fresh and frozen food dishes.

sage

Parsley is used for decoration, as well as in sauces.

The herb farmer also grows plants for other farms. One grower buys thousands of tiny sage plants; he grows them on, and then sells the sage to make sage and onion stuffing.

Another grower buys camomile plants. The oil from the flowers is used in making expensive perfumes.

camomile

Mint makes a good sauce to go with lamb.

Both are used in many Italian dishes.

oregano   marjoram

Basil is very popular in tomato salads as well as sauces.

Look in the shops for the more
unusual vegetables.
Farmers buy seeds from other countries
and experiment with growing them.
Sometimes these new vegetables from abroad
are difficult to sell because
people don't know how to prepare them.

squash

frisée endive

celeriac

lady's fingers

radicchio

fennel

Published by Dinosaur Publications 1988
8 Grafton Street, London W1X 3LA

Dinosaur Publications is an imprint of
the Children's Division, part of
the Collins Publishing Group

Text copyright © Althea Braithwaite 1988
Illustrations copyright © Jacqueline Wood 1988
All rights reserved

Printed by Warners of Bourne and London